SIGN LANGUAGE 3

SIGN LANGUAGE 3

Further Adventures in Unfortunate English
from the Readers of The Telegraph

SIGN LANGUAGE

First published 2013 by
Aurum Press Limited
74 – 77 White Lion Street
London N1 9PF
www.aurumpress.co.uk

Copyright © 2013
Telegraph Media Group

A catalogue record for this book is
available from the British Library.

ISBN 978 1 78131 171 4

Compiled by the team at
Telegraph Travel:
Senior Editor: *Oliver Smith*
Contributing Editors: *Natalie Paris,
Jolyon Attwooll*

10 9 8 7 6 5 4 3 2 1
2017 2016 2015 2014 2013

Design: Transmission
www.thisistransmission.com

Printed in China

CONTENTS

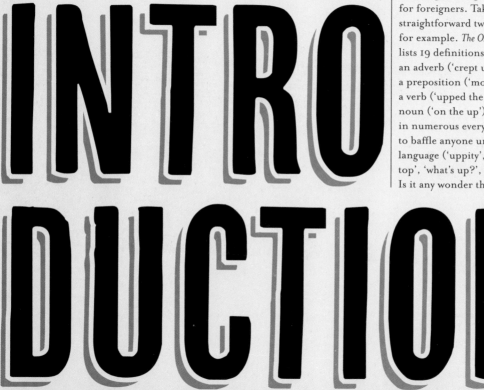

INTRODUCTION

The English language is a minefield for foreigners. Take the seemingly straightforward two-letter word 'up', for example. *The Oxford English Dictionary* lists 19 definitions for it. 'Up' can be an adverb ('crept up behind him'), a preposition ('move it up a bit'), a verb ('upped the ante'), and a noun ('on the up'), and it features in numerous everyday phrases likely to baffle anyone unfamiliar with the language ('uppity', 'up against it', 'up top', 'what's up?', 'up-and-coming'). Is it any wonder there are so many cock-ups when non-natives try to learn our mother tongue?

English is also ridden with idioms. Is any language that includes the phrases 'belt and braces', 'by a long chalk', 'kick your heels', 'paying through the nose' and 'a bone to pick' really worth the effort of mastering it?

Luckily for fans of *Sign Language*, much of the world has little choice but to try. English is the universal language of business, entertainment, and international diplomacy, and the spending power of British and American tourists cannot be ignored. And, equally fortunately, the results are often comical.

It was way back in 2008 that *Telegraph Travel* first asked its eagle-eyed readers to keep their peepers peeled for poorly spelled, mistranslated or simply incomprehensible signs during their overseas adventures. Gordon Brown was firmly ensconced at 10 Downing Street, Beijing was preparing to host the Olympics, Lehman Brothers was still seen as a bastion of sound financial investment, and the seeds of a sign-spotting phenomenon were being sown.

After making that tentative first appeal, we hoped for a handful of photographs at best. The response was little short of overwhelming.

Hundreds of submissions, from mangled menus in Marbella to nonsensical notices in Nairobi, arrived in our inbox, and we began publishing a weekly gallery on the *Telegraph* website, featuring our pick of the best.

Tuesday (chosen as it is widely considered the most depressing day of week) became *Sign Language* day at *Telegraph Travel* HQ, as the digital team gathered to chuckle at our readers' humorous offerings before we unveiled our favourites.

As the months passed, the tide showed little sign of slowing, and *Sign Language* was quickly established as one of the most popular online features, attracting upwards of 200,000 hits each week. And it's still going strong. We've received more than enough emails to publish a gallery of new images every Tuesday (without exception) for more than five years.

All of which serves to show that our love of twisted English and the world's over-reliance on poorly-programmed online translators remain equally undiminished by time.

Over the following pages we present – for the third year running – the funniest images from the last twelve months, as well as a few which were deemed too rude for publication on the *Telegraph* website (see 'X-Rated', page 142). Enjoy!

Send us your signs

Can you do better? Send your amusing and confusing signs to **signlanguage@ telegraph.co.uk**. See **telegraph. co.uk/signlanguage** for our terms and conditions and to see our weekly galleries.

AT YOUR SERVICE

There is an important rule in business. In a crowded market place, it pays to stand out.

For a shop, the key to drawing in customers is to have a front that grabs the shopper's attention. There are plenty of signs in this chapter that certainly do that. But whether they persuade English-speaking tourists to hand over their cash, as opposed to sniggering and reaching for their cameras, is another matter.

The brand, products or services on offer must also seem desirable, or at the very least, up to scratch. The medical practice Hope and Faith may not have too long a waiting list, for example.

Fashion boutiques should aim to present a style shoppers will aspire to – a reaction the signs for furniture store Sissy Boy and shoe shop Athlete's Foot may fail to inspire among English-speaking patrons.

So perhaps the second rule in business should be: if you want to attract international customers, employ a decent translator so you don't become a laughing stock.

Though one hopes that the business owners in these pages are having the last chuckle, as word about their services spreads to distant corners of the world via the pages of *Sign Language*.

MADMAN IN THE MIRROR →
Location: The Himalayas, Nepal
Spotted by: Louise Ross

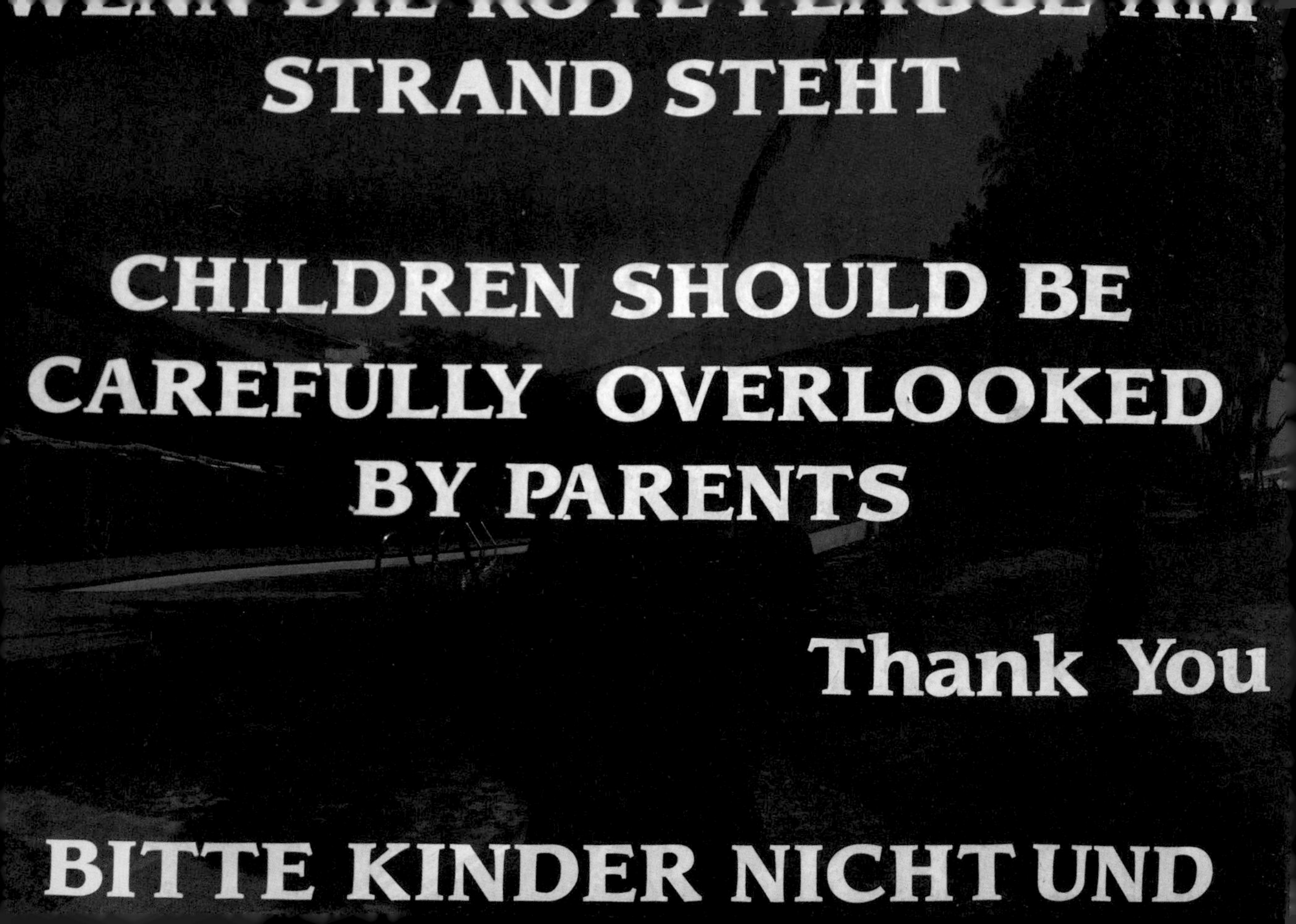

WENN DIE ROTE FLAGGE AM
STRAND STEHT

CHILDREN SHOULD BE
CAREFULLY OVERLOOKED
BY PARENTS

Thank You

BITTE KINDER NICHT UND

→ **PUSH OFF**
Location: California, USA
Spotted by: Steve Green

→ **SHOP 'TIL YOU POP**
Location: Shanghai, China
Spotted by: Stuart Pearce

← **DON'T LOOK NOW**
Location: Sri Lanka
Spotted by: Guy Dobson

← **FALLING STANDARDS**
Location: Ladies' boutique, Lech, Austria
Spotted by: Steve Green

→ **BIG IS BEAUTIFUL**
Location: Tanzania
Spotted by: Peter Griffiths

ANTIQUE TABLES
MADE DAILY

FURNITURE
SHOWROOM
OPEN

→ **ALL YOU CAN EAT**
Location: Kuala Lumpur, Malaysia
Spotted by: John Pinnick

→ **GAG REEL**
Location: Hastings, UK
Spotted by: Bob Hodges

← **MAKING HISTORY**
Location: Pennsylvania, USA
Spotted by: Karen Rorison

CADBURY
STD BARS

3 for
£1.50

Offer includes Cadbury Dairy Milk 49g,
Double Decker 60.5g, Twirl 34g, Wispa Gold 52g
and Cadbury Dairy Milk Chunks 56g.

← **BITTEN OFF MORE THAN YOU BARGAINED FOR?**
Location: petrol station, UK
Spotted by: Belinda White

→ **PURVEYORS OF DEODORANT**
Location: Nagoya, Japan
Spotted by: Malcolm Halcrow

→ DRESS TO DISTRESS
Location: Addis Ababa, Ethiopia
Spotted by: Colin Allen

→ CRACKING DEAL
Location: Aberdeen, UK
Spotted by: Sally McGrath

← GAP IN THE MARKET
Location: Littlehampton, UK
Spotted by: David Theobal

← **NOT FALLING FOR THAT ONE**
Location: Belgium
Spotted by: Ray Finlayson

→ **FASHION VICTIM**
Location: China
Spotted by: Ross Gash

小仙女
slavery

→ DIAGNOSIS: UNCERTAIN
Location: Hong Kong
Spotted by: Elaine Harris

→ SHOULD HAVE GONE TO...
Location: Dubai, UAE
Spotted by: Peter Hall

← NO REFUNDS
Location: Lantau Island, Hong Kong
Spotted by: Trevor Smith

← **SHOP 'TIL YOU DROP DEAD**
Location: unknown
Spotted by: Eugene Gannon

→ **HOME FURNISHINGS FOR REAL MEN**
Location: Amsterdam, Holland
Spotted by: Tim Campbell

→ **FOOL'S GOLD**
Location: Krakow, Poland
Spotted by: Stewart Jordan-Tubbs

→ **SATISFACTION GUARANTEED**
Location: Hotel in Suzhou, China
Spotted by: SJ Brooks

← **HO-HO-HORRID**
Location: Tondu, Wales, UK
Spotted by: James Davies

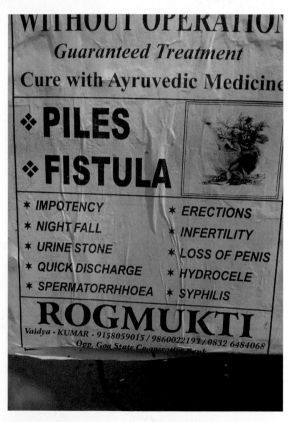

百姓眼镜

COMMON PEOPLE GLASSES

BIG S

定点验

阳朔县医疗保险

V

← **PAINT IT BLACK**
Location: Paris, France
Spotted by: John Hiscock

↑ **ALL YOUR CHRISTMASES COME AT ONCE**
Location: Japan
Spotted by: Donn Bierwerth

← **RUNNING GAG**
Location: Bandung, Indonesia
Spotted by: Chris Reece

→ **COAX HOAX**
Location: Madras, India
Spotted by: Hughie Coulter

ATTENTION!

Guests Are-Advised
To be CAUTIOUS
of Strangers at Hotels Around
Who Coax you for
A Dance-Party-or-Something Like
They are Troublesome

Manager,
BROAD LANDS-LODGING HOUSE
16, VALLABA AGRAHARAM STREET, TRIPLICANE,
MADRAS-600 005.

Phone : 845573
848131

ON THE ROAD

Buckle up sign lovers. Strap yourselves in tightly as we begin a voyage through *Sign Language*'s bread and butter: the road sign.

Whether it is the mighty kerbside billboard, a humble roadworks warning, or even a suggestive street name, this has been our meat, and yes, our two veg, since we first set out to explore the oddities of different notices across the globe. This seemingly innocuous branch of our linguistic travels has been our most steadfast category, the staple we could rely on through thick and thin.

Take the passenger seat, as you will find plenty of distractions en route. We'll stop off at Chuckleville, pass through Sniggerton, and meet the good folk of Guff-Orr. Prepare to rev your way up the Pun Highway, scoot down Smutty Lane (via Porte Arse), branch off Double Entendre Boulevard, enjoy a brief stay in Rectum and turn around at the odd dead end (where attractions include, yes, another cemetery). With a pinch of scatology and a dose of absurdity, we've got all the ingredients for a memorable voyage. This will be a road trip like no other, a breathless one-way journey between the twin towns of Mirth and Merriment. Enjoy the ride…

SIGHTS FOR SORE EYES →
Location: Niagara Falls, USA
Spotted by: Anthony Cooper

cataract tours
& SIGHTSEEING, INC.
CATARACT TOURS.COM
1-866-716-3255
16

1-866-716

RUE
PORTE ARSE

↑ **ALL'S WELL THAT...**
Location: Endwell, New York, USA
Spotted by: Bernie Grover

← **BACK STREET**
Location: Moissac, France
Spotted by: Malcolm Hipple

← SELF-PUBLICITY
Location: New Zealand
Spotted by: John Wilson

→ A VILLAGE THAT'S MAKING A SPLASH
Location: Asturias, Spain
Spotted by: John Price

APOLOGIES FOR
DELAYS
UNSTABLE BANK
BEING
INVESTIGATED

← **SIGN OF THE TIMES**
Location: Totnes, Devon, UK
Spotted by: Michael Williams

↑ **DON'T BANK ON IT**
Location: Goa, India
Spotted by: Yoko Pagels

← **FAMOUS FOR ITS SAUERKRAUT**
Location: Memmingen, Bavaria, Germany
Spotted by: Graeme Barker

→ **SHE'S VERY ACCOMMODATING**
Location: Franchhoek, South Africa
Spotted by: Neil Oakey

← **ROAD RAGE**
Location: Switzerland
Spotted by: Celia Soares

↑ **PARK AND DIE**
Location: Grantham, UK
Spotted by: Peter Bouch

← **BACK END OF BEYOND**
Location: Overijssel, The Netherlands
Spotted by: Steve McIlwrat

→ **POINTED REMARK**
Location: Mumbai, India
Spotted by: Julia Derrick

BEAUMONT SQAURE E1

LONDON BOROUGH OF TOWER HAMLETS

← **SHAPE UP!**
Location: London, UK
Spotted by: Jonathan Scott-Smith

↑ **GROT ROD**
Location: Kolkata, India
Spotted by: David Drew

← **IT'S A DUMP**
Location: Piran, Slovenia
Spotted by: Francis Trenado

→ **REDUNDANT NOTICE**
Location: Bromley, UK
Spotted by: Adrian Wyborn

← **HE WHO SMELLED IT SPELLED IT**
Location: Austria
Spotted by: Philip Budden

↑ **WHAT'S THE POINT?**
Location: Cuba
Spotted by: Kevin Crawford

← OPEN DOOR POLICY
Location: Johannesburg, South Africa
Spotted by: Paul Waudby

→ NOT ALL IT'S CRACKED UP TO BE
Location: Bangalore, India
Spotted by: Ian Hazlewood

11号敌楼
You Are Here

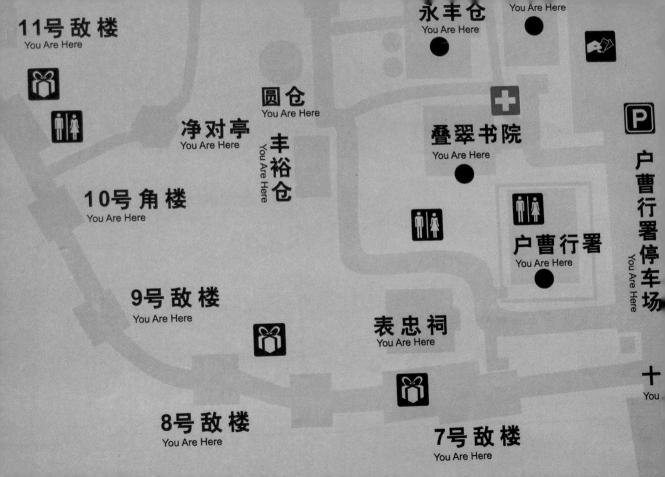

永丰仓
You Are Here

圆仓
You Are Here

净对亭
You Are Here

叠翠书院
You Are Here

丰裕仓
You Are Here

10号角楼
You Are Here

户曹行署停车场
You Are Here

户曹行署
You Are Here

9号敌楼
You Are Here

表忠祠
You Are Here

8号敌楼
You Are Here

7号敌楼
You Are Here

← **OMNIPRESENT**
Location: Great Wall of China, China
Spotted by: Dennis Tricker

↑ **POINTLESS POST**
Location: Northern Cyprus
Spotted by: Keith Hughes

← THE JOKER OF JEREZ
Location: Jerez Zoological Gardens, Spain
Spotted by: Trevor Pogue

→ BALLS-UP
Location: Harpenden, UK
Spotted by: Ronan Gelling

FAVOR ESPERE
POR EL PILOTO
PLEASE WAIT FOR
THE PILOT

← **THE TIPS OF THE ICEBERGS**
Location: unknown
Spotted by: Godfrey Holter

↑ **FLYING SOLO**
Location: Airport in Costa Rica
Spotted by: Colin Kerr

← **AIRWAY TO HEAVEN**
Location: Trondheim, Norway
Spotted by: Edward Sutton

→ **THE WINDY CITY**
Location: Oslo, Norway
Spotted by: Peter Norton

TOILET HUMOUR

Readers, it is time to take a trip to the Portaloo of puerility. This is a brand of wit which some may sniff at, but that's something we really wouldn't recommend.

Let's face it: we all need to relieve ourselves in the bog-standard world of toilet humour every now and then.

A dear friend of *Sign Language* recalls a family holiday, the finer points of which are hazed by the unkind ravages of the years. But one detail remains undimmed, defying the passage of time, that of the sign hovering above the poorly-chlorinated pit of water in the resort. 'Don't dive in the poo', it innocently instructed guests.

Who would have thought a missing consonant could provide such mirth? Even the parents of our mutual friend – a fine, upstanding, but reserved pair – could not keep their upper lips rigid as our hero and his siblings collapsed into fits of giggles every time they considered a dip.

The moral of this tale is this: resistance is futile, readers. Embrace the low-brow, irresistible lure of potty humour. Loo-se yourselves for a few moments (do forgive us). Yes, undo the latch, make yourself comfortable, and slide across the engaged sign. It is time to plumb new depths, as we take you on *Sign Language*'s magnificently crass close encounters of the turd kind.

NOISY NEIGHBOUR →
Location: USA
Spotted by: Charles Scholefield

GENTS
OPEN 8am to 9.30

"THE GUNPOWDER HOUSE"
PUBLIC TOILETS

These toilet facilities are currently unavailable.

Please make use of alternative facilities on the floor.

Group Property & Facilities

← **EXPLOSIVE**
Location: Isle of Man, UK
Spotted by: Keith Hughes

↑ **TIME TO SQUAT**
Location: Baker Street Underground Station, UK
Spotted by: Andy Davison

↑ NOT FOR REPRODUCTION
Location: Felbrigg Hall, Norfolk, UK
Spotted by: David Bass

→ UNITED URINATIONS
Location: Babbacombe Model Village, UK
Spotted by: Claudia Niblett

seventh
GENERATION®

100% Recycled Bathroom Tissue
Papier Hygiénique Recyclé

- Minimum 50% Post-Consumer Recycled Paper
- Whitened without Chemicals Containing Chlorine • No Added Dyes or Fragrar

4 Rolls/Rouleaux 2-ply/épaisseurs
4 in x 4 in (10.1 cm x 10.1 cm)

300 sheets per roll / feuilles par rouleau

金融广场
Financial Plaza

厕所 请下楼后转
Toilet Please walk downstairs and go backwards

← WASTE NOT, WANT NOT
Location: Ohio, USA
Spotted by: Brian Harrington

↑ CONTORTIONISTS' RESTROOM
Location: Shanghai, China
Spotted by: Tina Daubney

↑ **WHERE ELSE?**
Location: Royston Kite Festival, Hertfordshire, UK
Spotted by: Graham Tebby

→ **ITCHY BUSINESS**
Location: California, USA
Spotted by: Ian Dickinson

← BREEZY RIDERS
Location: Singapore
Spotted by: Bill Armstrong

↑ STANDING ROOM ONLY
Location: Mumbai, India
Spotted by: Matt

It's civilized to get close to urinate

↑ **SNUGGLE UP**
Location: China
Spotted by: Liz Ollier

→ **MAKING A SPLASH**
Location: Ice Hotel, Sweden
Spotted by: Nick Milnes

ArSeNet
Servicios en Internet

Servicio Técnico

→ CHEEKY
Location: Munich, Germany
Spotted by: Alan Bates

→ LAP OF THE BOGS
Location: London, UK
Spotted by: Ross Hayward

← WI-FFY
Location: Madrid, Spain
Spotted by: Adrian Hall

请勿将拖鞋穿入浴室
小 心 地 滑
Please get baboosh off
in the bathroom
Be careful landslip

↑ **SHOWERED WITH
NONSENSE**
Location: China
Spotted by: Sam Baird

→ **SURELY 'RUMP'?**
Location: Muscat, Oman
Spotted by: Tim Regan

GOBBLEDEGOOK

A few years ago the Chinese government launched a campaign aimed at eradicating the thousands of misspelled and poorly translated signs that litter the country's hotels, restaurants and tourist attractions.

'Chinglish' – the common term for China's own brand of linguistic lapses – was said to be harming the country's image. What would overseas visitors think of such ham-fisted attempts to communicate with the English-speaking world?

With tourism on the rise, new hotels opening nearly every day, and a population of more than 1.3 billion, the task appeared more arduous than painting the Forth Bridge. Judging by the following gems, the grammatical crusade was an utter failure.

This year, *Telegraph Travel* readers visiting the Far East have been advised to 'be exposed to rediation (sic)', 'scream the room', and 'be careful to steps'.

Notices intended to warn people to 'keep off the grass' were sighted with translations ranging from 'please with a single step of a bypass around grass you laugh laugh' to 'protect greening so as to endow benefit to descendents'.

And visitors to Fengdu were urged to 'pay attention to the upper air to fall the thing, the passing pedestrian forbid strictlys (sic) the stay'.

Similarly incomprehensible offerings were spotted beyond the Orient – in Cyprus, Turkey and Madeira, for example – but Asia provided the overwhelming majority of contributions for this chapter.

For giving us, and our readers, continued amusement, we thank the signwriters of China – as well as Japan, Burma and Thailand – and compel the Mandarins in Beijing to abandon their ill-advised campaign.

IF YOU CAN'T STAND →
THE HEAT
Location: Hurghada, Egypt
Spotted by: Spencer Hearne

If You Are
On Fire
Don't Run!

请您足下绕一绕
草儿向您笑一笑
Please With A Single Step Of A Bypass
Around Grass You Laugh Laugh

← **THE GRASSED LAUGH**
Location: Suzhou, China
Spotted by: Navjot Singh

↑ **SHOUT OUT**
Location: Zhouzhuang, China
Spotted by: Navjot Singh

THIS DOOR IS NOT A DOOR.

Please enter cafe via entrance on Platform 1.

← **OPEN AND SHUT CASE**
Location: Aberystwyth, UK
Spotted by: Rhys Davies

→ **GOING ROUND IN CIRCLES**
Location: Mae Hong Son, Thailand
Spotted by: James Cameron

The Circle of life, Grow old, Get ill and
Then Die So What's Going On In The Circle

滑りますので足元にご注意ください

Please be careful to steps.

お　願　い

夜間に虫が入ってきますので、
ドア・窓は閉めて頂きますようお願いします。

Please close window.
Because an insect enters in the night.

ご注意下さい。

機器点検のためこの扉が突然開くことがあります
お荷物などカウンターの上に置かれる時は落下の恐れがあり
ますのでご注意下さい。

Please note it.

This door might open suddenly for the equipment check.
Please note that there is fear of the fall when it is put on
the counter such as the spare pricks.

← THINGS THAT GO BUZZ IN
THE NIGHT
Location: Hokkaido, Japan
Spotted by: Anna Bramsdon

↑ WHAT'S THE POINT?
Location: Yudenaka Onsen railway station, Japan
Spotted by: Simon Castleman

DOLMUŞLAR HER 5 DAKİKADA BİR ALT YOLDAN GEÇMEKTEDİR.

1 OF 5 MINUTES DOWN THE ROAD LATE BUS TO THERE.

+4.00

HIGH-DEGREED SPECTACLE FOR READING DISCOMFORT

高度数老眼鏡

↑ **I CAN'T BELIEVE WHAT I'M SEEING**
Location: Tokyo, Japan
Spotted by: Adrian Jones

← **MAGICAL MYSTERY TOUR**
Location: Turkey
Spotted by: Kevin Shade

→ **BASCKET CASE**
Location: Uruguay
Spotted by: Jenny Rushforth

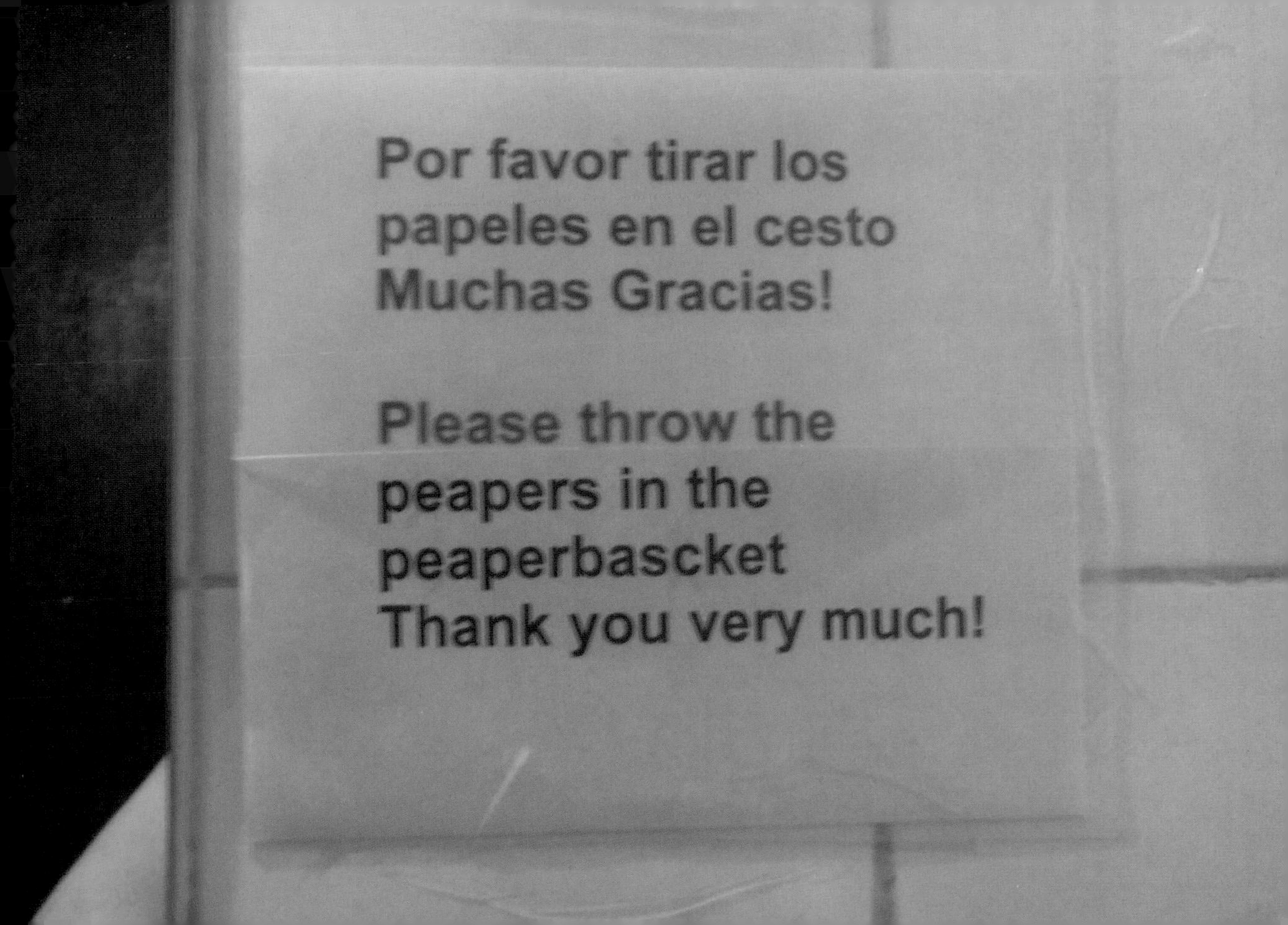

Por favor tirar los
papeles en el cesto
Muchas Gracias!

Please throw the
peapers in the
peaperbascket
Thank you very much!

赏长城美景 记烟火无情

APPRECIATE LOVELY VIEW OF THE GREAT WALL, DO NOT
FORGET THE FIRE IS HEARTLESS!

此处距停车场2170米 距旅游终点480米

THE DISTANCE TO PARKING LOT IS 2170 METERS.
TO TRAVEL TERMINAL POINT IS 480 METERS

SAFE SEX SHRINE

DROP IN AND MAKE A WISH
AT OUR WISHING WELL
(MOST REASONABLE WISHES WILL COME TRUE)

← **FIRE THE SIGN WRITER**
Location: Beijing, China
Spotted by: Kate Clode

↑ **WHAT THE WELL?**
Location: Bangkok, Thailand
Spotted by: Philip Hellawell

Dear Guests,

We would like to
inform
that there will be
an earthquake
at around 4:00 PM
today, according to
the weather forecast.

Thank you!!

注意高空坠物
过往行人严禁逗留
Please pay attention to the
upper air to fall the thing, the
passing pedestrian forbid
strictlys the stay.
成都市屹华建筑工程公司 宣

↑ **STRICTLY NONSENSE**
Location: Fengdu, China
Spotted by: Mike Atkins

← **ALL SHOOK UP**
Location: Burma (no earthquake occurred)
Spotted by: Andy McClelland

→ **LAUGHING IN THE AISLES**
Location: USA
Spotted by: David Hamer

Attention Shoppers: Due to manufacturing issues, we are currently out of good sense. We are sorry for any inconvenience.

BURNS THE CLOTHES BOARD
RED VALUABLY ENTERS WAN HOME
HAPPINESS ALSO IS NATURA
FOUR BIG MERITS
ARTISTIC RELIABLE IS PRACTICAL

Be exposed to rediation

← **HOT STUFF**
Location: Tajikistan bazaar
Spotted by: Chris Alexander

↑ **ALSO AVAILABLE: BLUE-RAYS**
Location: Osaka, Japan
Spotted by: David Millrine

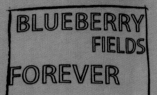

BLUEBERRY FIELDS FOREVER

let me take you down
cause i'm going to blueberry fields
nothing is real
and nothing to get hung about
blueberry fields forever

IS A SONG BY THE ENGLISH ROCK BAND

Protect greening so as to endow benefit to descendents

↑ **WELL ENDOWED**
Location: China
Spotted by: Colin Goldsack

← **WRITTEN BY JOHN LENIN**
Location: Bangkok, Thailand
Spotted by: Gavin Lazaro

→ **LOGIC YOU CAN'T FAULT**
Location: Tallin, Estonia
Spotted by: Jack Middleton

KOHT ON AVATUD, JUHUL, KUI EI OLE SULETUD

PLACE IS OPEN, IF IT IS NOT CLOSED

> hotel rule:
>
> * When you bring the animal for fondling in to the room. When you bring dangerous articles such as gunpowder, the gun, swords, and the poisons, and the thing that becomes troubled of other guests due to the stink in to the hotel.

← **BEWARE! KNOCK-OUT GAS**
Location: China
Spotted by: John Sacks

↑ **NO HEAVY PETTING, NO HEAVY WEAPONS**
Location: Tokyo, Japan
Spotted by: Rachel Tanner

AYAKKABI ve ÇANTA TAMİRHANESİ

AYAKKABI TAMİRİ
(Shoes Repair)

AYAKKABI DİKİMİ
(Shoes Planted)

TOPUK YAPIMI
(Hell of shoe construction)

BOT FERMUAR YAPILIR
(Zipper Bots Aree Made)

ORİJİNAL AYAKKABI BOYASI
(Shoe Shie)

ORTOPEDİK ASTAR
(Orthopedic Lining)

BIÇAK BİLEME

AYAKKABI AÇMA ve KALIP
(Parttern is shoes)

← 20 metre →

MANUAL REFUND	FOREIGN TOURIST QUATA		
	Train No.	Class	No. of Seat/Berth
विदेशी पर्यटक/Foreign Tourist	12001	CC	08
वरिष्ठ नागरिक/Senior Citizen	12279	CC 2S	04 04
समूह बुकिंग/Group Booking	14211	2S	10
स्वतन्त्रता सेनानी/Freedom Fighter	12137	SL	02

नोट : स्वयं के आने पर प्राथमिकता

① विदेशी पर्यटक

↑ **TWO SENIORS AND AN INSURGENT, PLEASE**
Location: Agra, India
Spotted by: Nick Peatson

← **A LOAD OF COBBLERS**
Location: Kyrenia, Cyprus
Spotted by: Colin Johnson

→ **AGE-OLD RECIPES**
Location: Beijing, China
Spotted by: Tim Campbell

FOOD AND DRINK

There's something about ordering food abroad that is always nerve-wracking. You've already had to deal with the stress of choosing a restaurant. Do you give in to the silver-tongued waiter trying to usher you in from the street or return to the tiny backstreet operation you passed in the hope that its 'authentic' menu will make up for its decor? Once you're seated things don't get any easier. Apologetic smiles don't always make amends for language failings in the way we hope they might.

But it's when the harassed waiter eventually presents you with a menu that the problems reach their peak. It's probably partly the fear of ordering the wrong thing that, after all the effort, makes badly translated menus so comical.

As you desperately scan the plastic-coated page for familiar dishes, anything with chips or, if all else fails, pizza, the odd and occasionally disgusting-sounding combinations stand out a mile. They also serve to make us feel better about what will eventually be brought to our table. Who cares if the sauce is too spicy or the steak a little chewy when a less thorough perusal of your options could have seen you eating 'good slag porridge' or 'crispy crap'?

NOT SO WHOLESOME →
Location: Beijing, China
Spotted by: Tom Swales

1031 棒渣粥　5元/碗
功效：补气健脾，健胃
Good slag porridge

冷采 | Cold Dishes

脂渣拌圆葱
Fat slag mixed with onion

32 元/例

蜜汁无核小枣
Seedless Dates with Honey

↑ **NO YOLK**
Location: Nicosia, Cyprus
Spotted by: Martin Hassett

→ **USE PROTECTION**
Location: Thailand
Spotted by: Peter Tomlinson

← **UNUSUAL DINNER DATE**
Location: 'Upmarket' restaurant, Qingdao, China
Spotted by: Stuart Keens

↑ **DUMP-LINGS**
Location: Taiwan
Spotted by: Catalina Magnusson

← **NOT AS BAD AS IT SOUNDS**
Location: Simferopol, Ukraine
Spotted by: Malcolm Brown

→ **BY THE BOWEL-FUL**
Location: Vienna, Austria
Spotted by: Charlotte Williams

5 Stk. 2,50 €

KNUSPRIGES KREBSFLEISCH
7 Crispy Crap 5 Pieces

5 Stk. 3,90 €

3,5

HUHN
8 Chi
with Noo

4,5

↑ **SO NICE THEY NAMED IT TWICE**
Location: Puntarenas, Costa Rica
Spotted by: John Duggan

→ **GRUMPY LENTILS**
Location: Dubai, UAE
Spotted by: Tim Campbell

← **A COFFEE BY ANY OTHER NAME**
Location: Zhongshan, China
Spotted by: Carl Barker

Cod & Chips, Bread &
Butter
A choice of tea or Coffee
£7.45 *May contain bones*

↑ **NO BONES ABOUT IT**
Location: UK
Spotted by: Mike Wareing

→ **RUDE FOOD**
Location: Perth, Australia
Spotted by: Frank Connor

EURO SHOPPER

VÍNO BÍLÉ

1 l

SK VÍNO BIELE
Víno zo Španielska.
Alk.: 11 % obj.
Informácie o alergénoch: tento výrobok obsahuje
oxid siričitý.
Výrobná dávka a dátum plnenia: uvedené na
vrchnej strane obalu.
Balí: FELIX SOLIS, S.L., R.E. CLM-081/CR01
Autovia del Sur Km 199, 13300 Španielsko

1 l

↑ **POACHED**
Location: Havana, Cuba
Spotted by: Neil McMillan

→ **A WHITER SHADE OF PEEL**
Location: UAE
Spotted by: Paul Beltrami

← **DELICATE PALATES BEWARE**
Location: Prague, Czech Republic
Spotted by: Sue Collins-Taylor

Vitamin C
whitening peeling cream
كريم تبييض وإزالة القشور من البشرة

برائحة البرتقال وفيتامين سي

Clean out horniness whitening

30 second dispel horniness
إزالة القشرة في 30 ثانية

← **IT'S ADDICTIVE**
Location: Sri Lanka
Spotted by: Gregor Carfrae

→ **WAITER! THERE'S A HAIR IN MY SQUID ROAST**
Location: Chiang Rai, Thailand
Spotted by: Ginny Summerlin

ร้านบุญรอดน้ำจิ้มรสเ

ปลาหมึกย่าง หอยแครงลวก/เ

ปลาหมึกย่างหนวดเล็ก
THE MOUSTACHE IS TINY SQUID ROASTS

ปลาหมึกย่างหนวดยักษ์
THE DEMON MOUSTACHE SQUID ROASTS

ปลาหมึกย่างหมึกกล้วย/หมึกไข่
THE BANANA SQUID/EGG SQUID ROASTS

หอยแ
THE AR

20   กุ้งเ
THE S

30-50   ลูกชิ้
70-100   THE

↑ NOT FISH AGAIN!
Location: British Columbia, Canada
Spotted by: Vernon Stradling

→ DYING TO GO
Location: Turkey
Spotted by: Rhiannon Williams

← CRUDE FOOD
Location: San Francisco, USA
Spotted by: Adrian Hall

↑ AND BURGER...?
Location: Route 66, USA
Spotted by: David Coates

→ SERVICE WITHOUT A SMILE
Location: Amsterdam, Holland
Spotted by: Tim Campbell

↑ **SLIM PICKINGS**
Location: Bath, UK
Spotted by: Paul Burgess

→ **THE BROWN SAUCE IS A WORRY...**
Location: Bangkok, Thailand
Spotted by: Ian Riches

← **SMELLS FISHY**
Location: Maui, Hawaii, USA
Spotted by: Will Raf

← WITH ALL THE TRIMMINGS
Location: New York, USA
Spotted by: Stan Gordon

→ À LA CART
Location: Istanbul, Turkey
Spotted by: Clare F Harve

Cabbaş...
Heart Salad
Patatoes Salad
Sausage Salad
Eggplant Salad
Yogurt Pasta
Şakşuka   7,50 tl
Yogurt Eggplant   10,00 tl
Feta Cheese Salad   7,50 tl
Tuna Fish Salad
Chicken Salad
Vicious
Shepherd Salad
Crushing Pain
Cacık

www.facebook.com/sportstreet.sk

PIZZA

V „CRAZY PUBE"
AREÁL HIER RADOST   50 m

four 4n

↑ **A MEAL AT WAR WITH ITSELF**
Location: Silver Spring, Maryland, USA
Spotted by: Craig Oakley

→ **PILING ON THE PRAWNS**
Location: Hong Kong
Spotted by: Angela Lishman

← **SHORT (AND CURLY) CRUST**
Location: Bratislava, Slovakia
Spotted by: David Jones

Ah, man's best friends. We love them, don't we? Them and the other members of the animal kingdom – the cast of horses, cats and other creatures – who we welcome into our hearts and homes.

We are a nation of softies, of pet-lovers who go gooey at the sight of a puppy filching our toilet paper, misty-eyed at the demise of a fictional cartoon deer. One recent study even suggested a quarter of pet owners refuse to go on holiday due to worries that something might befall their beloved pooch/moggie/guppy while they are away. It gets worse – another poll said most of us would rather cuddle our pets than our own flesh and blood.

Anthropomorphising is the word, if you're in a polysyllabic frame of mind. And so our signs suggest too. Yes, welcome to our menagerie of nature signs, of dogs that can't keep up the pace, poultry gone potty, lusty felines, nervous horses, sensitive octopus, and even of mad, bad peacocks. Aren't those animals funny when they fail to read the (human) script? Look at the horse who should be a bull, the swans ignoring the stop sign, and the arrow to the giraffe loo stop.

We wouldn't have it any other way, of course. The world of nature and pets offers such fertile ground for entertainment, even in the usually staid world of signs. It is almost, but not quite, worth missing a holiday for. Take it away, Fido and friends…

WHAT ABOUT THEIR DOGS? →
Location: Isle of Arran, UK
Spotted by: David Blackburne

NATURE

~ NOTICE ~

¡!
DOG OWNERS
DO NOT FOUL
ON TRACK OUTSIDE
HOUSE + WORKSHOP
NOTE - PENALTIES

↑ **FRISKY FELINES**
Location: Cervinia, Italy
Spotted by: Tim Eastmond

→ **FOWL PLAY**
Location: Muscat, Oman
Spotted by: Matthew Woolmer

← **WALKIES!**
Location: The Pilot Inn, Lyme
Regis, Dorset, UK
Spotted by: Phillip Stoneman

↑ WHAT IF IT'S A SHIH–TZU?
Location: unknown
Spotted by: Kevin Woodward

← TALKING BULL
Location: Wimpole Hall, Cambridgeshire, UK
Spotted by: Sean Grady

→ EIGHT-LEGGED EXPOSURE
Location: Monterey Bay Aquarium, California, USA
Spotted by: Tom Stevenson

Please don't flash
the octopus

HƯƠU CAO CỔ - NHÀ VỆ SINH
GIRAFFE - WC

↑ NO ROOM AT THE INN
Location: Luxor, Egypt
Spotted by: Mark Sharon

→ NEMO: FOUND
Location: London, UK
Spotted by: Andrea Lages

← LONG TALL LAVVY
Location: Ho Chi Minh City, Vietnam
Spotted by: Chris Howling

↑ **UN-STABLE**
Location: Devon, UK
Spotted by: Norbert Spichtinger

← **VENUS IN FEATHERS**
Location: Drakensberg, South Africa
Spotted by: Rod Parr

→ **NO KIDDING**
Location: Stellenbosch, South Africa
Spotted by: Sharon James

Beware of possible PEACOCK ATTACKS to cars

PARK AT YOUR OWN RISK

During mating season, peacocks display overt courting behaviour and have been known to attack reflective surfaces such as cars with polished bodywork. These territorial birds mistakenly view their own reflection as that of a competing peacock. The island's carparks cannot be protected from such free-ranging animals and drivers are advised that they park strictly at their own risk.

esident wildl

↑ NOT SO SECRET ANYMORE
Location: Devon, UK
Spotted by: Charlotte Lawrence

→ FLYING FILLIES
Location: Park Royal Hotel in Penang, Malaysia
Spotted by: Brian Aldridge

← FEATHER DUST-UP
Location: Sentosa Island, Singapore
Spotted by: Julia Derrick

← **NEIGH ENTRY**
Location: Wales, UK
Spotted by: JBR Davies

→ **MIRROR, CYGNET, MANOEUVRE**
Location: Isle of Man, UK
Spotted by: Keith Hughes

X-RATED

There is something about British humour that revels in saucy innuendo, rude jokes and plain old smut. Why? Is it our buttoned-up attitude and tendency to repress desires that lead to guilty feelings we can only relieve with humour? Maybe. We often hear that we live in a world of plunging moral standards, desensitised to the base and provocative stimuli thrown at us from all angles. Still, from the seaside postcards with their buxom lovelies and giant sticks of rock, to the raised eyebrow and knowing titter of Kenneth Williams in the *Carry On* films, indirect references to sex by way of double entendres retain the sure-fire propensity to amuse.

For some reason, sniggering at body parts and the merest hint of hanky panky (the phrase alone goes a long way to summing up the British mentality) will never grow old.

It's no surprise then that foreign signs with salacious and risqué English meanings make us titter. These bad translations are given added comedy value because they are unintentional.

This is a selection of the rudest, most blush-worthy signs that our readers have had the audacity to send us.

So set aside your otherwise high-minded view of the world, imagine Sid James is sitting cackling on your right shoulder and let your mind wander as we reveal the dirtiest *Sign Language* entries the publishers would allow us to print.

TOSSED TO THE CELLS →
Location: Nevada, USA
Spotted by: Michael H Caplan

พร สนุ๊กเกอร์
Porn Snooker

← CUE BALLS
Location: Chiang Mai, Thailand
Spotted by: Chris Sandar

↑ RINGING WITH LAUGHTER
Location: Wollaston, UK
Spotted by: Rich Beardsall

← **REEL MATURE**
Location: Florida, USA
Spotted by: John Mucklow

→ **HEAD TO THE END**
Location: Mont St Anne, Quebec, Canada
Spotted by: Annick van der Schoot

← **COFFEE OR BUST**
Location: Bangkok, Thailand
Spotted by: James Cameron

↑ **SOLD IN PAIRS**
Location: unknown
Spotted by: John Sproat

← I'LL HAVE WHAT SHE'S HAVING
Location: Kenya
Spotted by: Jai Pandit

→ IS EVERYTHING HANDMADE?
Location: Palma, Majorca, Spain
Spotted by: Alastair Harries

**← A GOOD PLACE TO
SPEND A PENNY**
Location: near Wrexham, UK
Spotted by: Patrick Blochle

↑ AN HONEST POLITICIAN
Location: Romania
Spotted by: name withheld

Capricci al Ragu' d'Anatra
Euro 8,00
Pates courtes au ragout de canard
Pasta quills with duck ragout
Makkaroni mit entenragout

*Tagliolini alle Erbe Fini
euro 8,00
Tagliolini aux fines herbs
Tagliolini with aromatic herpes
Tagliolini mit Gewurzkrauter

Ravioloni di Magro
Euro 8,00
Raviolis de ricotta et èpinards
Ricotta cheese & spinach ravioli
Ricottakase-u.spinat-Ravioli

← **ITCHING FOR SECONDS**
Location: Bieno, Italy
Spotted by: Chris Webb

→ **FORM A QUEUE**
Location: Bangkok, Thailand
Spotted by: David Sim

บางซื่อ
Bang Sue

2
ชานชาลา
Platform

ไปบางซื่อ
To Bang Sue

Cửa Hàng Bến Thành

Bán đúng giá niêm yết
Always sell at printed prices

Phục vụ ân cần
Whorehearted service

N ÁO
TRANG

ION
HING

VALI
TÚI XÁCH

SUITCASE,
HANDBAG

QU

← WHERE EVERY NOVEL HAS
A HAPPY ENDING
Location: Cape Town, South Africa
Spotted by: Kelly Jameson

↑ SERVICE WITH A SMILE
Location: Saigon, Vietnam
Spotted by: Ron Manley

↑ HE'S A SMOOTHIE
Location: Poland
Spotted by: John Martin

→ A VERY HANDS-ON BUSINESS
Location: Hong Kong
Spotted by: Richard Frampton

← **FRESHLY SQUEEZED**
Location: Southall, UK
Spotted by: Catalina Magnusson